Every Man is an army veteran and a recluse, preferring solitude to people. He suffers with P.T.S.D. (Post-Traumatic Stress Disorder).

This book is dedicated to the American Legion Post #37 and to all who served in a time and a place called Vietnam. And to others who served in abandoned causes.

# Every Man

## Soldier's Poems

AUSTIN MACAULEY PUBLISHERS™

LONDON • CAMBRIDGE • NEW YORK • SHARJAH

**Ordering Information**
Quantity sales: Special discounts are available on quantity purchases by corporations, associations, and others. For details, contact the publisher at the address below.

**Publisher's Cataloging-in-Publication data**
Man, Every
Soldier's Poems

ISBN 9798886937886 (Paperback)
ISBN9798886937893 (ePub e-book)

Library of Congress Control Number: 2024905921

www.austinmacauley.com/us

First Published 2024
Austin Macauley Publishers LLC
40 Wall Street, 33rd Floor, Suite 3302
New York, NY 10005
USA

mail-usa@austinmacauley.com
+1 (646) 5125767

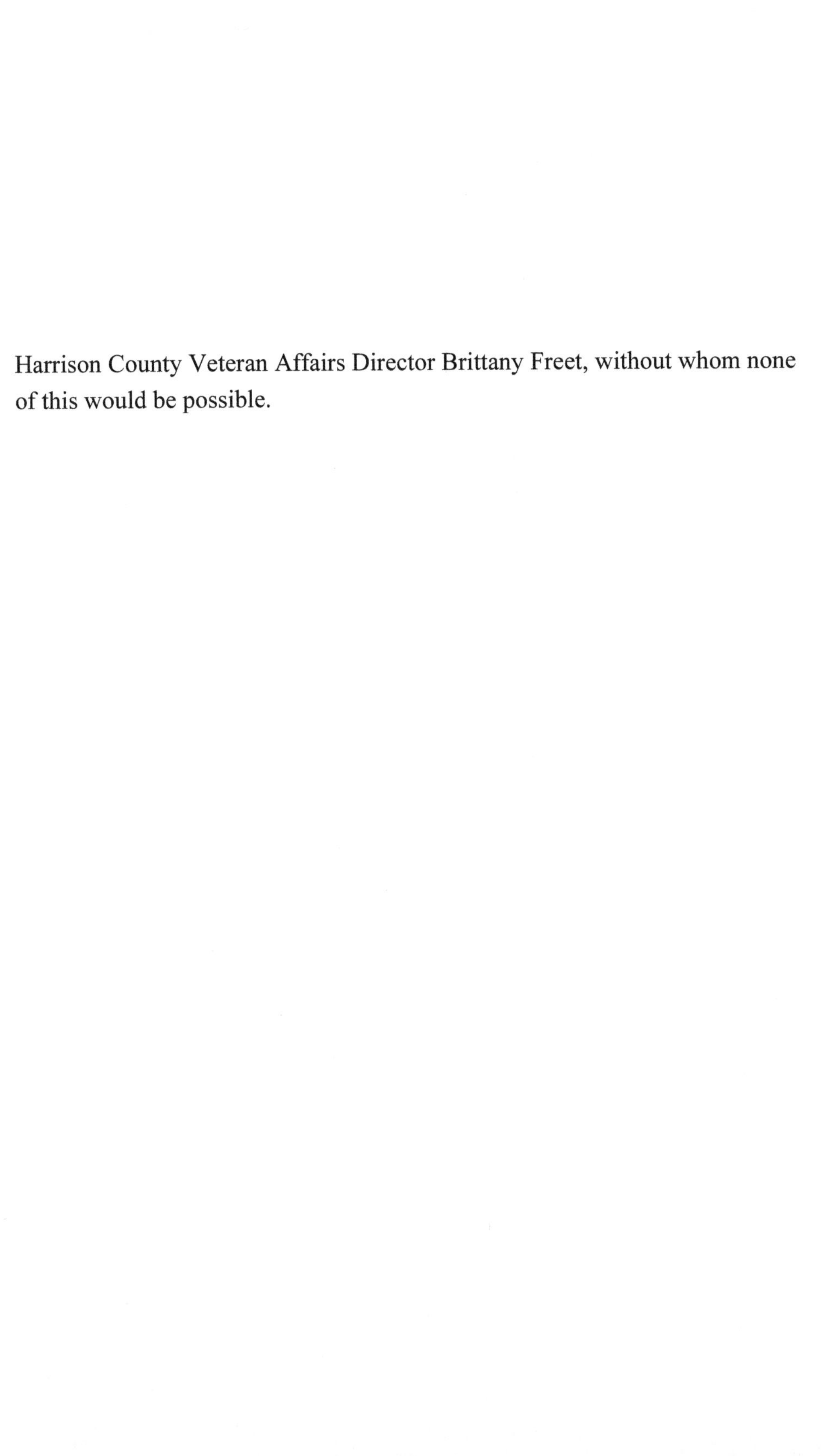

Harrison County Veteran Affairs Director Brittany Freet, without whom none of this would be possible.

# Table of Contents

# Vet

# A Statement

I am a Veteran of Vietnam.
I know you're not impressed.
You look at me and you see,
A killer,
A doper,
Maybe a bum?
Well, I have killed, that is true.
To save my life or my friends.
For you see I was proud to do my duty.
While most of you found a way to stay out.
I couldn't help what happened there.
But still you say it is my fault.
I tried to save lives,
Red, Yellow, Black, and White.
But for their side they did not
Care about a child's life.
I guess the joke is on me,
And all those like me.
They said they gave us parades
But I didn't see or hear about them
Because of the scenes and the noise
The protesters made.
But you do not have the right
To criticize me because I know
How you lived
And you can't say the same
To me.

# Mike's Poem

I load the planes.
I know what they carry.
There are bombs in the belly.
I know they will kill many,
But I do this work
So my brothers may live.
I feel it isn't much,
But all my time I give.
At sea, we fear nothing
But I hear of the war.
Many men being wounded,
Bodies shattered and torn.
Why do I worry?
I don't know for sure.
All I know is I want to do more.
The E-2's fly in and I help fill them out.
And when we are done,
The load master shouts.

# Red Sun

In the east, there is a land
It is said the sun is red.
It testifies to those who are dead.
A country that only knows hate.
Led by few with power great.
I see this land in my dreams.
My feet feel wet as I cross its streams.
Fire fills the sky.
Men scream and cry.
The corpsman yells, T
his one is dead.
He moves to the others lying ahead.
Pray for me, sweet Jesus
I hear to my right.
Shoot that damned gun, boy
This is a fire fight.

# Listen

Three friends went to smoke.
It was very dark.
It was very quiet.
Nothing outside, they said.
They looked,
but they couldn't see.
One remembered,
the sergeant said,
Never three,
Please listen.
Never three.
Never three in a match.
He smiled.
A lighter they used.
Each drew a cigarette,
Each began to draw,
drawing on the flame.
Something broke the quiet.
Two friends.
Neither smoke at night.
A sniper can see well at night.
No, young fools,
Deaf fools,
All he needs is a light.

# Alone I Sit

Alone I sit
in the dark.
The dark is my friend.
The dark makes me feel safe.
No one can see me
if I am quiet.
No one can hear me
If I stay
in the dark.
I am invisible
if I stay in the dark.
I am untouchable
if I stay in the dark.
I am invincible.

# Crys

Oh children
I am sorry
I want to hold you
I am not mean
but I can't
for you might kill me.
Because others are mean
they use you to hurt me.
They use your tiny hands
they set you down with wires attached.
There is evil in this land.
I want to save you
but I can't
I am here for a short time
my home is far away.
I will go back
but I will remember you;
you will be in my thoughts
the rest of my life.
I will pray for you
and for your mother's loss
or your mother lost from you
and curse the name of Charlie
the evil
which stole your life
and ruined your land.

# M.I.A.

Here I am walking dead
not knowing who I am.
I feel no life
as I walk,
only the pain
after death.
Who am I?
Please tell me.
I have a right to know
because it is for you
that I am here.
Now I cry for I am alone.
You say you don't know me.
I am sorry for that
because I died for you
and you don't remember
the place I was at.

# Fire Fight

The point man is down.
Take cover.
You up front,
get your head up.
Send out a 203,
There over there.
Sixty team,
Hit that tree over there,
There damn it.
Check yourselves.
Check your buddy.
All right pack up,
It's over.

# The Fourth of July

The Fourth of July,
A celebration.
Rockets red glare,
Bombs bursting in air.
Children with sparklers,
Big kids with M-80s.
Black cats firing
One string after another.
A week before,
A week after
It is hard to sleep.
I shake.
She watches.
She wants to know.
She does not ask.
Over ten years, she never asks.
To the park we go
To watch the fireworks.
The sounds of battle.
She gently touches me.
What do you see?
She wants to know.
Star bursts, napalm, tracers.
Mostly just fire.
She shakes.

# John Wayne

John Wayne
Said it
In a movie.
He said
When
A man
takes a weapon
And uses it,
Even
In battle.
The man
Can't help
But
Carry guilt.
The man
Who wrote
Those words
For John Wayne
To say
Was right.
I wonder
If he knew
How right
He was.

# See Me

God, why can't they look at me
and see who's standing there?
Why can't they see it's a man?
A good man that's trying
to do good.
Why do they see what they
see?
I am not a vision of dark
sickening images.
I am a man of many accomplishments.
I have pursued the dreams of
America,
and have been left wondering
what happened to the dreams
of America.
Isn't this where a man can be anything?
And isn't this where people
help their fellow man be anything?
Where are all those who are
supposed to be so caring?
I've looked and searched
but I don't see them anywhere.

# My Weapon

Where is my weapon?
Why do I need it?
Is it really for killing?
Is it to save my life?
Is it not a decoration?
Is it not pretty?
My weapon is in my hand.
I know why I need it.
It really is for killing.
It is for saving my life.
It is not a decoration.
It is not pretty.
I need it, but
I am scared of its power.
I am scared of weapons.

# Killer

We took prisoners,
we didn't kill them.
Why did you kill yours?
I use my weapon
when I have to.
I don't like to.
You think it's great,
being able to kill.
I know killing is easy.
But for your life,
you have to live,
live you will,
but with memories.
You make us look bad.
Killer,
I hate knowing you.
Killer, how can you help
when all you do
is hurt.

# Farmer?

A farmer stood in a field
He sowed no crops.
His father was farming, he was sure
Four rows at a time.
His father would be planting
He could not remember farming.
He could not if he tried
For now, he is a hunter
They made him a hunter.
He is hunting in a field
The field is filled with rice.
His farm has pigs and cows
This has snakes and tigers.

# Point Man

To the front
walks a man.
Many, many lives
he carries.
Point man,
walk carefully.
 If you don't,
what will
we see
through elephant grass?
He leads us,
knowing
V.C. may
see us.
Rank, he seldom wears.
Bank our lives
in him
we will.
His eyes are sharp,
always narrow,
brave as the eagle.
He moves easy,
like a sparrow.
We believe
in him.
We must.
I know
in his job,
God
he does
trust.

# Cobra

In the sky
flies a serpent.
Its mouth
gaping open,
baring its teeth
for all.
Blood drips
from its
fangs.
Emerald green
is the skin
but dull,
no luster.
This serpent
spits fire
as it flies.
Always hungry
for more
prey.
Its eyes
never close.

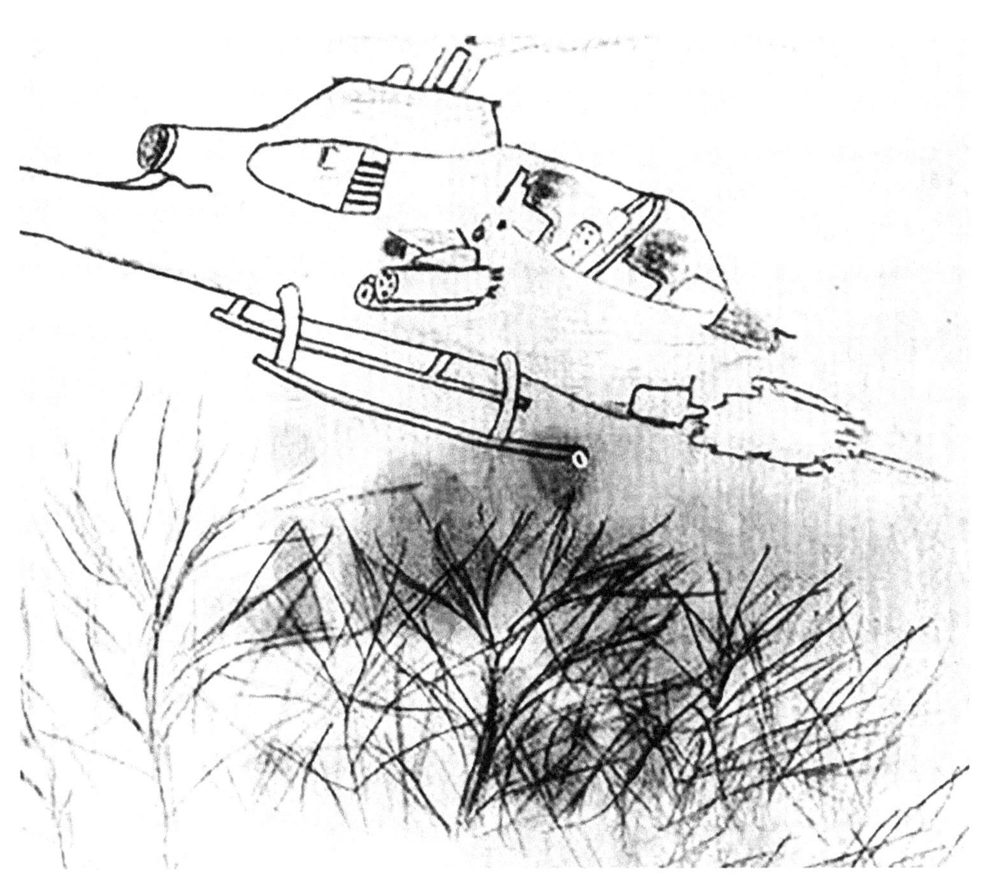

# Tired

I'm sorry, Sarge, I can't
I can't go anymore
The sweat is running
The sweat is stinging my eyes
We cut and we cut
And we cut some more
I cut so much bush
I can't cut any more.

# Night Patrol

It is dark out here.
Where are we headed?
Did you ever notice
in the movies
the good guys
see good at night?
"Quiet back there;
if we can't see Charlie,
that means he can't see us."

# Thoughts

What the hell is this?
Walking around out here.
We're not doing a damn thing.
Mosquitoes
Tigers
Pungy stick pits.

A worn green jacket
Hangs
On the back
Of a chair.
A black E-5
Chevron pin
Tacked to
The collar
In the corner
Lays
A hat

It too is Green
A broad brim
Encircles
The crown
The things
That remind s
The only
Things that
Remain
Besides
Memories.

A soldier
Stands
In the rain
It's Christmas
He reads
The
Stars and Stripes
Peace talks
Paris
He believes
For two
Months
They were in
Paris

And now
They
Went home
But
I'm still here
Because
They argued
Over a table
My mother
Would have
Gave them
Her own.

I am
Feeling
So bad
Do you
See that
Lord?
I am
Away
From her
And she

Says she
Loves me
No more.

I know
You can
Change her
And when,
From battle
I return
Perhaps,
She will
Love me more
For she
Will have
A year
To learn.

I want to fight.
God damn it.
I want to fight.
I just can't
Sit
and get
Pounded
Any more.
What the hell
is this?

Why can't
We move?
There's no
God damn wall Sit
That
Holds us.
Just some
Stupid
Invisible
Line.

A ghost
Haunts me.
It is invisible
To everyone
But me.
They cannot
See it,
Hear it,
Or feel it.

But I know
It is there
The ghost
That haunt
Me,
Is the ghost
Of my
Past.

All right, dig in.
Two-man L.P.s
Get those trees cleared.
Goddamn it,
Won't they let us rest?
Little bastards.
I'm hungry.
I'm tired.
I'm hit.
He's dead.

# Scout

Scout,
Are you brave?
Are you crazy?
How many days does it take for your mission?
Expendable you are.
They don't care.
But if you don't come back,
They won't go in there.

# Tribute

Warriors without horses
charging a flaming sky,
Men rounded in honor
without causes
praying not to die.
Men who were in battle
lost to glory and time
I wonder why
their heads
are held so high.
Remember a land
where the sun is blood red;
working for freedom
in a country
already dead.
I wonder why
they don't cry.
For freedom is a way
for them
to live and die.
Duty
is their search
for truth
while fighting
horrid lies.
I wonder
at their
heads
held so high.
Where are they now
the ones who survived
the past?
They're living in hometowns
waiting

to heal at last.
They're waiting to know
why
they were denied.
They're waiting to know
why
their friends
had to die.
I wonder why
their heads
are held so high.
They're waiting for a time
when people
really understand
they did not
forsake anyone
or their homeland.
They're hoping
When the smoke
of battle clears
they will let them
shed their tears
and help them cry
saying please
hold your head
up high.
For freedom
is a way for them
to live and die.
duty
is their search
for truth
while fighting
horrid lies.
I wonder
at their
heads
held so high.

# The Uniform

In the closet
Hanging far in back
Is a uniform.
Small hands find it.
Small fingers trace its
Arrangement. Small eyes soak in the
Many colors on a field of dark
Green.
Small feet run to find Daddy.
Small lips utter the question
Daddy, were you a soldier?
Small ears listen for reply
Small explosions erupt in
Daddy's
Mind.

# Die Hard

They tried
To kill us
But we
Kept coming
Because
We were mad
we were tired
we were hungry
They had us
Pinned down
I saw
Some of
Their faces
They were smiling
But those
Faces lost
Their grins
When we
Came
I screamed
We screamed
Yelling
At the tops
Of our lungs.
When my
Weapon was
Empty
I swung it.
I didn't care
Kill me,
You little
Bastards
Come on
Kill me

They didn't
They couldn't
They were scared
They didn't
Believe
We could
Take them
We didn't
Believe it
Either.

# Home Ward Bound

The point man lead
It was our squads turn
We took our turn
Four times,
In a row.
The Captain said
We had to
Make contact
Before we came back in.
The point man lead
He tripped a wire
But
It didn't go off
On the point man.
But it did
Go off
On him.
He fell back
Holding his stomach
We grabbed his hands,
He didn't have
A stomach.
"Mommy, it hurts."
"My tummy hurts."
"Mommy."
"Help me, Mommy."
"Mommy."
"Mommy."
"MOMMY."
"Call a chopper."
"Get him bagged."
"You know something?"
"What?"
"I want my mom."
"Yeah, me too."

# No One Wants a Hero

No one wants a hero.
I know.
I'm a hero.
Heroes have honor.
No one knows honor.
Heroes have faith
Do they know faith?
Heroes search.
They don't find.
Heroes give.
They take.
Heroes must help.
For that
is what
a hero is to do,
But,
no one wants a hero.
Damn shame.

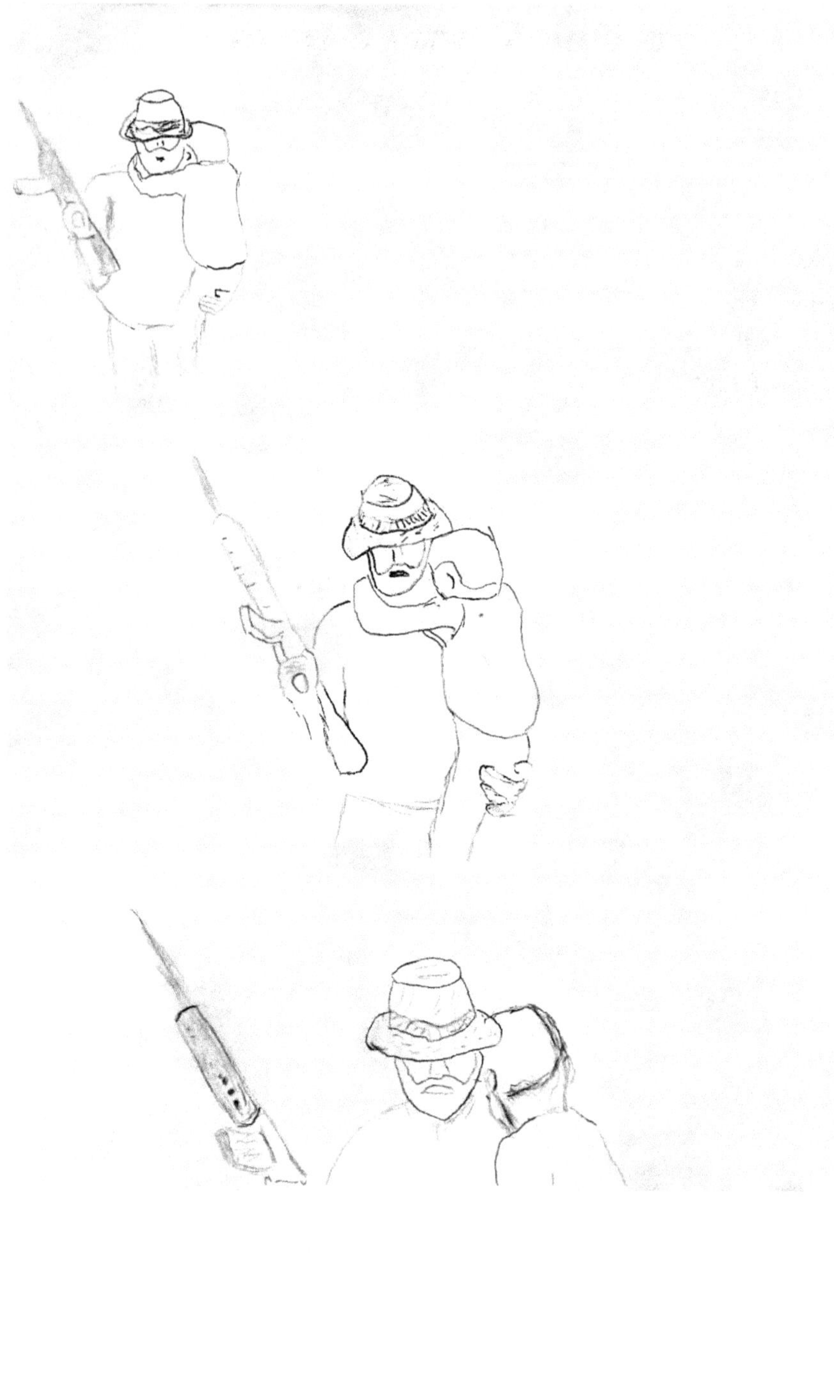

# What Is the Price of Freedom?

What is the price of freedom?
I should like to know.
Is it the bloody death in battle,
a body separated from its soul?
Is it shouting and cursing
men do across a table?
Is it the many mechanical creatures
hidden in a forgotten stable?
Is it a child crying
for its mother who is dying?
Perhaps it's all the things
I have mentioned,
but why must we always go
 in such a violent direction?
We always say,
"Oh God, why?"
But in his own words he told us
It is up to us how to die.
So what is the price of freedom?
Is there such a land,
where a man does not have to fight
the grip of a giant hand?
Perhaps the price is
a body separated from its soul
its spirit being free to float along
with heaven as its goal.

# "The Rock"

Trust in the Lord Jesus Christ
He is the rock of your
Salvation.

After the Chaplain finished
with that.
We should have been
brave as Hell.

Hill 209 was not a Hill.
It was steep
and seemed to be
a Mountain.

We went up
and we went back
down.

Third time we got
halfway up.

I hid behind a Rock
but it was not Jesus
it was just a
Goddamned Rock.

Christ was a Co-Pilot
on an E-vac Chopper
I was sure of that.

# "Lucky You"

You got drafted
and didn't
have to go.
Ho!
Ho!
Ho!
Ho!
Ho!
Ho!
Ho!

# "No More"

Congress said,
Not another
Vietnam.
Kuwait?
Afghanistan?
Iraq?
Syria?
Not
Another
Vietnam
So what about
Peace
In
our time?
Never say Korea.

# "Tunnel Rat"

Tunnel Rat, you can't
look back.

Down you go
into that dark
hole.

Getting back out
is a good goal.

Up top
the air is clean.

.45 in hand
you do not feel mean.

Just scared,
anxious
to get out of that
lair.

# "MO" Draft Board

Gone for two years.
Prominent citizens.
Bankers.
Dealership Owner.
Rich Farmer.
They chose.

They went;
Gone two years.

Banker
"I haven't seen you for
quite a while.
Where have you been?"

MO
"You don't know
where I have been?"

Banker
"Should I?"

MO
"You're the son of a bitch
that sent me to Vietnam and
you don't remember?"

# "Never Got Settled In"

They don't know me
They don't understand.

Three wives
Three divorces

It's your fault
all the way though
Even if they lied
and
Cheated on you.

They asked
what you wanted
and you told
them too.

But they didn't
like what they
heard.

So shame
on you.

# "Coming Home"

Coming home
was like I never
left.

Nobody cared
what I wanted
to get off
my chest.

Nightmares
Night sweats.

Help with
chores.

Don't drink
that beer.

Don't talk
about whores.

Don't say
fuck
all the time.

Like you did
when you asked
for the peas
at supper time.

# "P.T.S.D"

Always watching,
Super alert.
Always dreaming,
Nightmares while sleeping.
Just want to be
Left alone.
Always tired.
Don't share
With those who
Were not there.
Divorce.
Three wives gone
From over
40 years
of Maylay.

# "Lesson Learned?"

Asha Valley
Operation Apache Snow
Eleven days
May 9–May 20, 1969
Abandoned June 6, 1969
72KIA
370 Wounded
Korengal Valley
Entered 2004
Operation Red Wing
June 28, 2005
Operation Avalanche
October 2007
Abandoned April 4, 2010
54KIA
Several hundred wounded
Just asking.

# "Purple Heart"

Hopper was on the sixty
when they
Hit the wire.
He melted
a barrel.
Broke it off
and threw on
another.

Next day.
"Hey, Hopper.
How did
last night go?
Laying on
his bunk.
"Alright,"
he said.
"Heard you had
a close one."
"That kid feed's
stuck his head up, said he
 couldn't see 'em."
"Did he get hit?"
"No, just my hand
when I pushed him down."

# Dios Te Amo Hermana Dios Te Amo

When you get to heaven, if you do
That's probably when you'll get a clue.
Some are smart, smarter, or more
gifted than you.
Also, others have feelings too.

He wasn't in Vietnam.
He never heard the A-Ks song.
He never saw an N.V.A
He was feeling sorry for himself
Slopping chow on someone's tray.
He's so sensitive, being picked on for being a cook.
Maybe it's time for another look.

All he does is talk people down
and you also, why do you get to look down on others.
Your religion says they are your sisters and brothers.

Christ didn't come for the perfect like you.
He came for the sinners like me.
Read your bible you'll see.

All these years you have made yourself appear great.
I remember when you broke that soapbox crate.

He never saw chu-hoy
He was also a big Momma's Boy.
You're the only ones that hurt.

The only ones who suffer loss.
You ask for prayers
And say get lost.

# Another War

I heard the news
The Russian Army has attacked Ukraine
To me, the news was bad.
Some laughed, not me.
I saw the video lapse.

Putin thought he'd
blow away Ukraine.
They didn't wish
Their lives to change.
They're fighting back very hard.
Not sure when it will all collapse.

The Russian Army kills little kids,
rapes their mothers too.
They kill them big or small.
I see no end to it all.

The world needs Russians oil
The U.N. doesn't know what to do.
The world needs oil
So the food won't spoil.

They say the Putin is wrong.
But the war goes on and on.
Now it's nuclear weapons
Putin threatens to disperse.
All I want to do it curse.
This world needs peace.
All countries hostilities should cease!

# "No More"

Congress said
Not another
Vietnam.
Kuwait?
Afghanistan?
Iraq?
Syria?
Not
Another
Vietnem
So what about
Peace
In
Our time?
Never say Korea.

# Religions

Abraham
Is the
Father
Of Three
Religions
That all
Want to
And Have
In
The
Name
Of
His
God
Killed

# Hate Is Great

Hate
Is great
Love
Is a
Four letter
Word
Like
Turd
S ###
P ###
F ###
Let's
Be
Polite
Defecate
Urinate
Fornicate
Charity
Has yet
To
Trump
Hate
Charity
Doesn't
Mean
Love
Anymore
It Means
Giving
What
One is
Comfortable
With

# Common Ground

Mothers
Cry for their kids
Black
White
Red
Yellow
Buddhist
Christian
Muslim
Jewish
A mother
No Matter
What faith
No matter
What Color
So why
All the
Hate?

# Ethnic Cleansing

A seventeen-year-old girl hung in Kosovo in the name of it and religion. Unite people of the world, it could be for any of us to experience. It ended the Sergeant Rock comic book, *Make War No More*.

# A Comment

As I think and write about world events both past and present. I feel helpless to make anything that transpired right or the future better. The United Nations need to unite. The countries that want peace need to sue for it, sadly fight for it. Russian and Chinese annexation is not right. If there are people there before you it belongs to them, period.

China does not need Taiwan; Russia does not need Ukraine. Imperialism is not good. Annexation just gets people killed. What kind of leaders start illegal wars that steal countries and lives? Great leaders should sue for peace and truth. The egos of monsters need to be subdued. It's the peacemakers that are blessed.

The people of the world need to look up and out to space. That is where a global threat may come from. The world leaders and governments rule arbitrarily. Never putting the populous first. Let's cure diseases, pollution, and hunger. Russia and China could lead in the world in that.

The aged, women and children, not just soldiers are dying from annexation. Please, Russian, stop! Please, China, don't start! All religions say they are peaceful, prove it. Governments and leaders tell the truth. Leaders fight your own damn war and leave everybody else out of it. Putin, you want Ukraine. Then arm yourself and go take it. Just you, by yourself. Xi Jining, you do the same for Taiwan. Let everybody else live.

The world needs compassion and peace. Not dominance. Future world leaders, sue for peace and go on to prosperity and good health for your countries and the world. Go green!